Sardar Vallabhai Patel: Quotes

His Mind, His Thoughts

31 October 2022 (147th Birth Jayanti of Sardar Patel)

Compiled & Edited by

Badri Narayan Krishnan

NOTION PRESS

NOTION PRESS

India. Singapore. Malaysia.

Contents

Bheema of the Freedom Struggle

C. Rajagopalachari, close associate of Sardar Vallabhai Patel said:

"Vallabhbhai was to Gandhiji exactly what Lakshmana was to Shri Rama."

As an avid lover of the Indian Freedom Struggle, I believe, if not for his early death on 15 Dec 1950, Sardar Patel was destined to be a Prime Minister of India.

We know he led the team to unite India. Even more momentous was his leadership in uniting the Freedom Struggle. Gandhi was his absolute sworn leader, but he united the varied ideologies of Ambedkar (Dalit), Subash Chandra Bose (Socialist/Armed struggle), Jinnah (2 Nation), Nehru (Modern atheist), the Communists, Hindu Mahasabha, the RSS and many more.

I hope this peek into his thoughts gives you an insight into this Gentle Giant son of Bharat Matha.

Praphrasing was necessary for clarity, language & context. Paraphrased quotes are marked (*)

Badri Narayan Krishnan,

31 October 2022 (147th Birth Jayanti of Sardar Patel)

Acknowledgments

This being a compilation stands on the shoulders of many historians, academics, news articles, Sardar Patel NVIL Library (http://sardarpatel.nvli.in) and more. Gandhi Bhawan (Mysore University), Mysuru Swatantra Horatagarara Sangha and my friend Karthikeyan have inspired me immensely to this task.

I heartily thank all of them.

All copyrights remain with the rightful owners.

Badri Narayan Krishnan

31 October 2022 (147th Birth Jayanti of Sardar Patel)

1. India & Patriotism

"Hyderabad is in my hands"
(When the Nizam of
Hyderabad refused to join
the Indian Union)

"A nation's greatness is reflected in the character of her people" (*)

"Accepting and adopting a National language is a service to India" (*)

"We have to banish untouchability and live like the children of the same father" (*)

"Hindi, the National language should be as wide as the ocean, in which all the languages of India take its own proper place" (*)

"There is something unique in this soil, which despite many obstacles has always remained the abode of great souls"

2. War & Peace

"Our way is straight and clear—the building up of a socialist democracy at home with freedom and prosperity for all, and the maintenance of world peace and friendship with all nations"

"One can take the path of revolution but the revolution should not give a shock to the society. There is no place for violence in revolution"

"Hyderabad is in my hands"
(When the Nizam of
Hyderabad refused to join
the Indian Union)

3. Religion & Caste

"Religion is a matter between the man and his Maker"

"No distinctions of caste
and creed should hamper us.
All are the sons and
daughters of India"

"The proof, if any proof is needed, is Hindu- Muslim unity... Similarly, we have established cordial relations with Parsis, Christians and other citizens of the country"

"There are some young men who believe that in this country there should be Hindu Raj and that Hindu culture alone has a place in India. Gandhiji was fighting against that mad idea....he said our salvation depended on unity"

"Caste, community
boundaries hamper our
growth. We have to speedily
forget all these thing" (*)

"Today we must remove distinctions of high and low, rich and poor, caste or creed"

"We have to develop the sense of equality and banish untouchability. We have to live like the children of the same father" (*)

4. Democracy in India

Jawaharlal Nehru Aug 15, 1947- May 27, 1964	Gulzari Lal Nanda* May 27-Jun 9, 1964	Lal Bahadur Shastri Jun 9, 1964- Jan 11, 1966	Gulzari Lal Nanda* Jan 11-Jan 24, 1966	Indira Gandhi Jan 24, 1966- Mar 24, 1977	Morarji Desai Mar 24, 1977- July 28, 1979
Charan Singh July 28, 1979- Jan 14, 1980	Indira Gandhi Jan 14, 1980- Oct 31, 1984	Rajiv Gandhi Oct 31, 1984- Dec 2, 1989	Vishwanath Pratap Singh Dec 2, 1989- Nov 10, 1990	Chandra Shekhar Nov 10, 1990- June 21, 1991	P. V. Narasimha Rao June 21, 1991- May 16, 1996
Atal Bihari Vajpayee May 16-June 1, 1996	H. D. Deve Gowda June 1, 1996- Apr 21, 1997	Inder Kumar Gujral Apr 21, 1997- Mar 19, 1998	Atal Bihari Vajpayee Mar 19, 1998 - May 22, 2004	Manmohan Singh May 22, 2004- May 26, 2014	Narendra Modi Sworn in on May 26, 2014

"In a democratic set-up we must have freedom of the Press, freedom of speech, freedom of expression and freedom of association and all kinds of freedom"

"Every citizen of India must remember that he is an Indian and he has every right in this country but with certain duties"

"True democracy or the swaraj of the masses can never come through untruthful and violent means"

"The rule of law should be respected so that the basic structure of our democracy is maintained and further strengthened"

5. Socialism

25

"The economic issues are most vital for us and it is of the highest importance that we should fight our biggest enemies - Poverty, unemployment"

"Give work to those who are
hungry, food to invalids,
forget your quarrels"

"My only desire is that India should be a good producer and no one should be hungry, shedding tears for food in the country"

"Today we must remove distinctions of high and low, rich and poor, caste or creed"

"Religion is a matter
between the man and his
Maker"

6. Satyagraha & Freedom

"Ours is a non-violent war, It is Dharma YUDDHA"

"India will not be benefited by brutal force. If India is to be benefited it will be through non-violence"

Chauri Chaura Incident

"The stiffer the opponent the more should our affection go out to him. That is the significance of Satyagraha"

"Gandhi's ten lines had greater force than a hundred- page memorandum"

"As satyagrahis we should always claim and we did – that we are always ready to make peace with our adversaries"

"A war based on Satyagraha is always of two kinds. One is the war we wage against injustice and the other we fight against our own weaknesses"

"Satyagraha is not a creed for the weak or the cowardly"

"Non-violence has to be observed in thought, word and deed. The measure of our non-violence will be the measure of our success"

"One can take the path of revolution but the revolution should not give a shock to the society. There is no place for violence in revolution"

Chauri Chaura Incident

"The war started by Mahatmaji is against two things – the Government and secondly against one self. The former kind of war is closed, but the latter shall never cease. It is meant for self-purification"

"Our way is straight and clear—the building up of a socialist democracy at home with freedom and prosperity for all, and the maintenance of world peace and friendship with all nations"

"True democracy or the swaraj of the masses can never come through untruthful and violent means"

"There are some young men who believe that in this country there should be Hindu Raj and that Hindu culture alone has a place in India. Gandhiji was fighting against that mad idea....he said our salvation depended on unity"

"It was after meeting Gandhi in 1917 that I was motivated to quit my job and join the Independence struggle" (*)

7. Freedom Fighters

"Gandhi's ten lines had greater force than a hundred-page memorandum"

"Jawaharlal and I have been devoted followers of the Great Master, soldiers in the struggle for freedom, fellow-members of the Congress, colleagues in the Congress" (*)

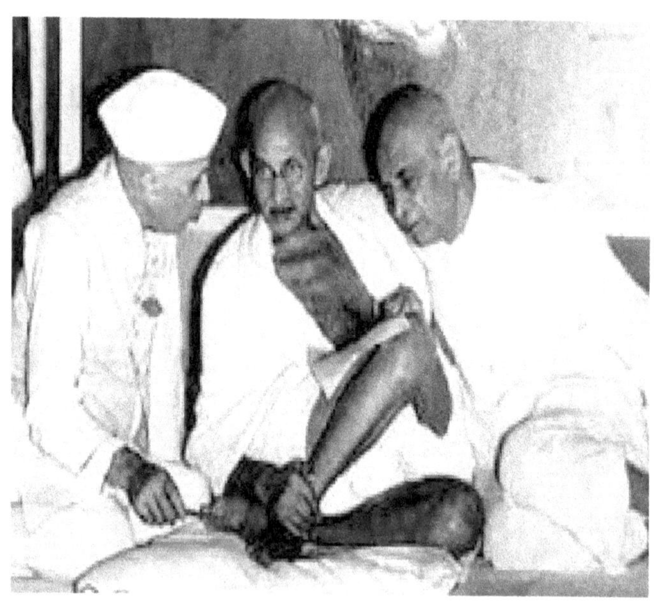

"The Great Master has unhappily left Jawaharlal and I to battle with grave problems without his guidance" (*)

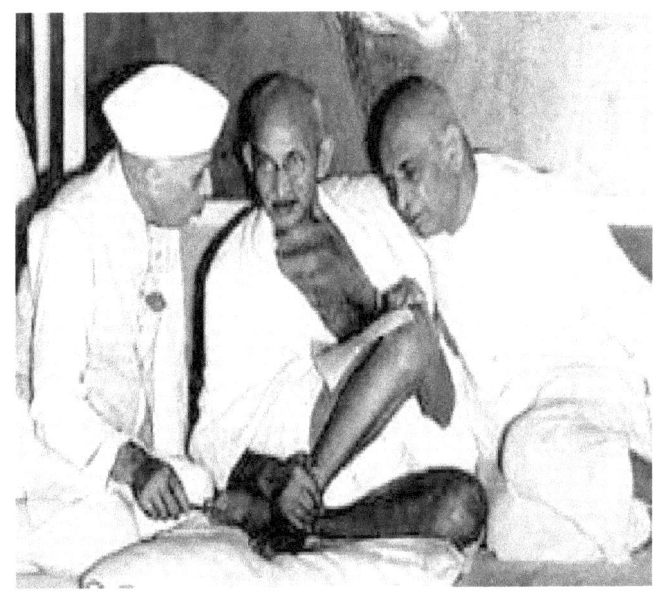

"My nearness, intimacy and brotherly affection to Nehru make it difficult for me to sum him up" (*)

8. Humor & Life

"Work is undoubtedly
worship but laughter is life"

"Anyone who greets joys
and sorrows with equal
facility can really get the
best of life"

"Let iron (enemy) be hot. Hammer (us) has to remain cold. Else it would harm itself" (*)

"When a meeting was disturbed by buffaloes grunt noises " even buffaloes are making speeches" (*)

"How can I avoid hurting ants while walking, someone asked. "Tell him to walk with his feet on his head." Sardar joked" (*)

"I have locked my brain and given the key to Gandhiji"

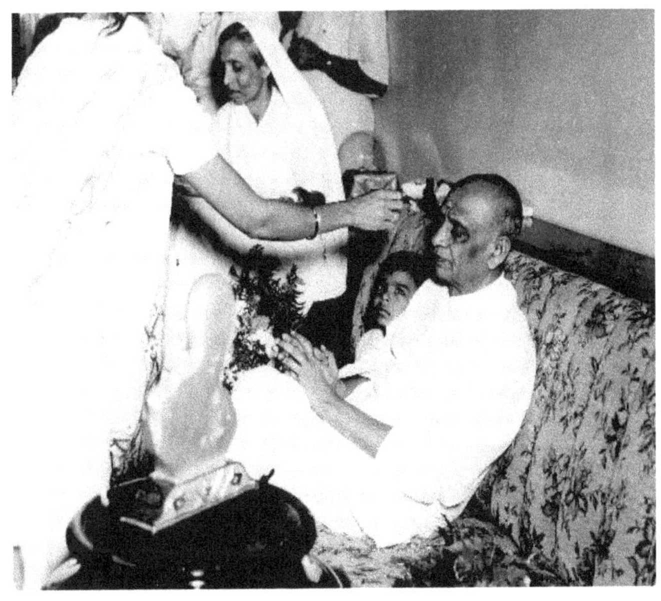

"I am "chaff among wheat" of the freedom leaders" (*)

"Character development is education.
Mere Bookish Knowledge is not education" (*)

Epilogue

Great humans have many dimensions: Religious & Atheist, Traditional & liberal, Emotional & strategic...

They challenge our ability to rise above our pettiness to learn from them.

Bheema of India, Sardar Vallabhai Patel is definitely one of them.

I would love to hear your thoughts, inputs, criticisms.

Badri Narayan Krishnan

Badrinarayan.11@gmail.com

www.ingramcontent.com/pod-product-compliance
Lightning Source LLC
Chambersburg PA
CBHW040108150726
48005CB00013B/1623